In the Year 1989

by

Kerry Butters.

In the Year 1989

Millennium: 2nd millennium

Centuries: 19th century – **20th century** – 21st century

Decades: 1950s 1960s 1970s – **1980s** – 1990s 2000s 2010s

Years: 1986 1987 1988 – **1989** – 1990 1991 1992

1989 (MCMLXXXIX) was a common year starting on Sunday (dominical letter A) of the Gregorian calendar, the 1989th year of the Common Era (CE) and *Anno Domini* (AD) designations, the 989th year of the 2nd millennium, the 89th year of the 20th century, and the 10th and last year of the 1980s decade. It was a historical turning point as a wave of revolutions swept the Eastern Bloc, starting in Poland that summer with the beginning of a move towards private enterprise, coming to a head with the opening of the Berlin Wall in November, embracing the overthrow of the communist dictatorship in Romania in December, and ending in December 1991 with the dissolution of the Soviet Union. Collectively known as the Revolutions of 1989, they heralded the beginning of the post–Cold War period.

It was the year of the first Brazilian presidential elections in 29 years, since the end of the military government in 1985 which commanded the country for more than twenty years, and marked the redemocratization process's final point. F. W. de Klerk was elected in South Africa, and his regime gradually dismantled the apartheid system over the next five years, culminating with the 1994 election that brought jailed ANC leader Nelson Mandela to power.

The first commercial Internet service providers surfaced in this year, as well as the first written proposal for the World Wide Web and New Zealand, Japan and Australia's first Internet connections. The first babies born after preimplantation genetic diagnosis were conceived in late 1989, starting the era of designer babies.

Contents

Events

January

- January 2 – Prime Minister Ranasinghe Premadasa takes office as the third President of Sri Lanka.
- January 4 – Gulf of Sidra incident (1989): Two Libyan MiG-23 "Floggers" are engaged and shot down by 2 US Navy F-14 Tomcats.
- January 7 – Hirohito dies, and Akihito is enthroned as the 125th Emperor of Japan immediately, followed by the change in the era name from Showa to Heisei on the following day.
- January 8 – Kegworth air disaster: A British Midland Boeing 737 crashes on approach to East Midlands Airport, leaving 47 dead.
- January 10 – In accordance with United Nations Security Council Resolution 626 and the New York Accords, Cuban troops begin withdrawing from Angola.
- January 11 – President of the United States Ronald Reagan delivers his farewell address to the nation.
- January 15
  - Thirty-five European nations, meeting in Vienna, agree to strengthen human rights and strengthen East-West trade.
  - A pro-democracy demonstration in Prague is attacked by the police.
- January 17 – Stockton schoolyard shooting: Patrick Edward Purdy kills 5 children, wounds 30 and then shoots himself in Stockton, California.
-

- January 18
  - The Polish United Workers' Party votes to legalize Solidarity.
  - Ante Marković succeeds Branko Mikulić as Prime Minister of Yugoslavia.
- January 20 – George H. W. Bush succeeds Ronald Reagan as the 41st President of the United States of America.
- January 23 – A powerful earthquake in the Tajik Soviet Socialist Republic kills around 275 people.
- January 23–24 – Armed civilian leftists briefly attack and occupy an Argentinian army base near Buenos Aires.
- January 24 – Florida executes Ted Bundy by electric chair for the murders of young women.
- January 29 – The British children's television show, *Thomas & Friends*, begins airing in the U.S. with the series premiere of *Shining Time Station* on PBS.
- January 30 – Prime Minister of Canada Brian Mulroney shuffles his cabinet, appointing 6 new ministers and reassigning the responsibilities of 19 others.

February

- February 1 – Joan Kirner becomes Victoria's first female Deputy Premier, after the resignation of Robert Fordham over the VEDC (Victorian Economic Development Co-operation) Crisis.
- February 2
  - Soviet war in Afghanistan: The last Soviet Union armored column leaves Kabul, ending 9 years of military occupation since 1979.
  - Carlos Andrés Pérez takes office as President of Venezuela.
  - Satellite television service Sky Television plc is launched in Europe.
- February 3
  - A military coup overthrows Alfredo Stroessner, dictator of Paraguay since 1954.
  - After a stroke, P. W. Botha resigns his party's leadership and the presidency of South Africa.

- February 6 – The government of the People's Republic of Poland holds formal talks with representatives of Solidarity movement for the first time since 1981.
- February 7
  - The People's National Party, led by Michael Manley, wins the Jamaican general election.
  - The Los Angeles City Council bans the sale or possession of semiautomatic firearms.
- February 10
  - Ron Brown is elected chairman of the Democratic National Committee, becoming the first African American to lead a major United States political party.
  - U.S. President Bush meets Canadian prime minister Mulroney in Ottawa, laying the groundwork for the Acid Rain Treaty of 1991.
- February 11 – Barbara Harris is the first woman consecrated as a bishop of the Episcopal Church in the United States of America (and also the first woman to become a bishop in the worldwide Anglican Communion).
- February 14
  - Union Carbide agrees to pay US$470 million to the Indian government for damages in the 1984 Bhopal disaster.
  - *The Satanic Verses* controversy: Ayatollah Ruhollah Khomeini, Supreme Leader of Iran (d. June 3), issues a fatwa calling for the death of Indian-born British author Salman Rushdie and his publishers for issuing the novel *The Satanic Verses* (1988).
  - The first of 24 Global Positioning System satellites is placed into orbit.
- February 15
  - Soviet war in Afghanistan: The Soviet Union announces that all of its troops have left Afghanistan.
  - Following a campaign that saw over 1,000 people killed in massive campaign-related violence, the United National Party wins the Sri Lankan parliamentary election.

- February 16 – Pan Am Flight 103: Investigators announce that the cause of the crash was a bomb hidden inside a radio-cassette player.
- February 17
  - The Arab Maghreb Union (AMU) is formed.
  - South African police raid the home of Winnie Mandela and arrest four of her bodyguards.
- February 20 – In Canada's Yukon Territory, the ruling New Democrats narrowly maintain control of the Yukon Legislative Assembly, winning 9 seats vs. the Progressive Conservative Party's 7.
- February 23 – After protracted testimony, the U.S. Senate Armed Services Committee rejects, 11–9, President Bush's nomination of John Tower for Secretary of Defense.
- February 23–27 – U.S. President Bush visits Japan, China, and South Korea, attending the funeral of Hirohito and then meeting with China's Deng Xiaoping and South Korea's Roh Tae-woo.
- February 24
  - The funeral of Hirohito is attended by representatives of 160 nations.
  - *The Satanic Verses* controversy: Iran places a US $3-million bounty on the head of *The Satanic Verses* author Salman Rushdie.
  - After 44 years, the Estonian flag is raised at the Pikk Hermann tower in Tallinn.
- February 27 – Venezuela is rocked by the Caracazo, a wave of protests and looting.

March

- March – Poland begins to liberalize its currency exchange in a move towards capitalism.
- March 1
  - The Berne Convention, an international treaty on copyrights, is ratified by the United States.

- A curfew is imposed in Kosovo, where protests continue over the alleged intimidation of the Serb minority.
- Louis Wade Sullivan and James D. Watkins start terms of office as U.S. Secretary of Health and Human Services and U.S. Secretary of Energy respectively.
- The Politieke Partij Radicalen, Pacifistisch Socialistische Partij, Communistische Partij Nederland and the Evangelical People's Party amalgamate to form Netherlands political party GroenLinks (GL, GreenLeft).
- After 74 years, Iceland ended its prohibition on beer; celebrated since as *bjórdagur* or beer day.
- March 2 – Twelve European Community nations agree to ban the production of all chlorofluorocarbons (CFCs) by the end of the century.
- March 3
  - Jammu Siltavuori abducts and murders two 8-year-old girls in the Myllypuro suburb of Helsinki, Finland.
  - Portugal wins the FIFA U-20 World Cup, defeating Nigeria on the final by 2–0 in Riyadh, Saudi Arabia.
- March 4
  - Time Inc. and Warner Communications announce plans for a merger, forming Time Warner.
  - The Purley station rail crash in London leaves 5 dead and 94 injured.
  - The first ACT (Australian Capital Territory) elections are held.
- March 7 – Iran breaks off diplomatic relations with the United Kingdom over Salman Rushdie's *The Satanic Verses*.
- March 9 – Revolutions of 1989: The Soviet Union submits to the jurisdiction of the World Court.
- March 13
  - A geomagnetic storm causes the collapse of the Hydro-Québec power grid. Six million people are left without power for 9 hours. Some areas in the northeastern U.S. and in Sweden also lose power, and aurorae are seen as far as Texas.

- o Tim Berners-Lee produces the proposal document that will become the blueprint for the World Wide Web.
- March 14
  - o Gun control: U.S. President George H. W. Bush bans the importation of certain guns deemed assault weapons into the United States.
  - o Christian General Michel Aoun declares a 'War of Liberation' to rid Lebanon of Syrian forces and their allies.
- March 15 – Israel hands over Taba to Egypt, ending a seven-year territorial dispute.
- March 16 – The Central Committee of the Communist Party of the Soviet Union approves agricultural reforms allowing farmers the right to lease state-owned farms for life.
- March 17
  - o The Civic Tower of Pavia, built in the 14th century, crumbles down.
  - o Alfredo Cristiani is elected President of El Salvador.
- March 20 – Australian Prime Minister Bob Hawke weeps on national television as he admits marital infidelity.
- March 22
  - o Clint Malarchuk of the NHL Buffalo Sabres suffers an almost fatal injury when another player accidentally slits his throat.
  - o Asteroid 4581 Asclepius approaches the Earth at a distance of 700,000 kilometers.

The *Exxon Valdez*

- March 23 – Stanley Pons and Martin Fleischmann announce that they have achieved cold fusion at the University of Utah.
- March 23–28 – The Socialist Republic of Serbia passes constitutional changes revoking the autonomy of the Socialist

Autonomous Province of Kosovo, triggering 6 days of rioting by the Albanian majority, during which at least 29 people are killed.
- March 24 – Exxon Valdez oil spill: In Alaska's Prince William Sound, the *Exxon Valdez* spills 240,000 barrels (38,000 m^3) of oil after running aground.
- March 27 – The first contested elections for the Soviet parliament result in losses for the Communist Party.
- March 29 – The 61st Academy Awards are held at the Shrine Auditorium in Los Angeles, with *Rain Man* winning Best Picture.

April

- April 1
  - Margaret Thatcher's new local government tax, the Poll tax, is introduced in Scotland.
- April 2
  - In South-West Africa, fighting erupts between SWAPO guerrillas and the South West African Police, on the day that a cease-fire was supposed to end the South African Border War according to United Nations Security Council Resolution 435. By April 6, nearly 300 people are killed.
- April 4
  - A failed coup attempt against Prosper Avril, President of Haiti, leads to a standoff between mutinous troops and the government which ends April 10, with the government regaining control of the country.
  - In Brussels, Belgium, NATO celebrates its 40th anniversary.
- April 5 – The Polish Government and the Solidarity labor union sign an agreement restoring Solidarity to legal status, and agreeing to hold democratic elections on June 1.
- April 6 – National Safety Council of Australia chief executive John Friedrich is arrested after defrauding investors to the tune of $235 million.
- April 7 – The Soviet submarine K-278 Komsomolets sinks in the Barents Sea, killing 41.
-

- April 9
  - Georgian demonstrators are massacred by Red Army soldiers in Tbilisi's central square during a peaceful rally; 20 citizens are killed, many injured.
  - A dispute over grazing rights leads to the beginning of the Mauritania–Senegal Border War.
- April 11 – Ron Hextall becomes the first goaltender in NHL history to score a goal in the playoffs.
- April 14 – The U.S. government seizes the Irvine, California, Lincoln Savings and Loan Association; Charles Keating (for whom the Keating Five were named) eventually goes to jail, as part of the massive 1980s savings and loan crisis which costs U.S. taxpayers nearly $200 billion in bailouts, and many people their life savings.
- April 15
  - The death of Hu Yaobang sparks the beginning of the Tiananmen Square protests of 1989.
  - The Hillsborough disaster, one of the biggest tragedies in European football, claims the life of 96 Liverpool supporters.
- April 17 – Poland, Solidarity is again legalized and allowed to participate in semi-free elections on June 4.
- April 19
  - Trisha Meili is attacked while jogging in New York City's Central Park; as her identity remains secret for years, she becomes known as the "Central Park Jogger."
  - A gun turret explodes on the U.S. battleship *Iowa*, killing 47 crew members.
- April 20 – NATO debates modernising short range missiles; although the U.S. and U.K. are in favour, West German Chancellor Helmut Kohl obtains a concession deferring a decision.
- April 21 – Students from Beijing, Shanghai, Xi'an, and Nanjing begin protesting in Tiananmen Square.
- April 23 – Zaid al-Rifai resigns as Prime Minister of Jordan in the wake of riots over government imposed price hikes that began on April 18.

- April 25
  - Noboru Takeshita resigns as Prime Minister of Japan in the wake of a stock-trading scandal.
  - The term of Baginda Almutawakkil Alallah Sultan Iskandar Al-Haj ibni Almarhum Sultan Ismail as the 8th Yang di-Pertuan Agong of Malaysia ends.
  - Motorola introduces the Motorola MicroTAC Personal Cellular Telephone, then the world's smallest mobile phone.
- April 26
  - Sultan Azlan Muhibbudin Shah ibni Almarhum Sultan Yusuff Izzudin Shah Ghafarullahu-lahu, Sultan of Perak, becomes the 9th Yang di-Pertuan Agong of Malaysia.
  - Zaid ibn Shaker succeeds Zaid al-Rifai as Prime Minister of Jordan.
  - The Daulatpur–Saturia tornado, the deadliest tornado ever recorded, kills an estimated 1,300 people in the Dhaka Division of Bangladesh.
- April 27 – A major demonstration occurs in Beijing, as part of the Tiananmen Square protests.
- April 28 – Pope John Paul II begins a 9-day trip to Madagascar, Zambia, Malawi, and Réunion.

May

- May – Transhumanism – Genetic modification of adult human beings is tried for the first time, a gene tagging trial.
- May – The Soviet Union issues its first Visa card in a step to digitalize its banking system.
- May 1
  - Andrés Rodríguez, who had seized power and declared himself President of Paraguay during a military coup in February, wins a landslide election in a general election marked by charges of fraud.
  - Disney-MGM Studios at Walt Disney World opens to the public for the first time.
  -

- May 2
  - The first crack in the Iron Curtain: Hungary dismantles 150 miles (240 km) of barbed wire fencing along the border with Austria.
  - The coalition government of Prime Minister of the Netherlands Ruud Lubbers collapses in a dispute about a pollution cleanup plan.
- May 3 – Cold War – Perestroika – The first McDonald's restaurant in the USSR begins construction in Moscow. It will open on 31 January 1990.
- May 4 – Oliver North convicted on charges related to the Iran–Contra affair. His conviction was thrown out on appeal in 1991 because of his immunized testimony.
- May 6
  - Yugoslavia wins the Eurovision Song Contest in Lausanne with the song *Rock me* performed by Riva.
  - Magnum XL-200 opens at Cedar Point amusement park in Sandusky, Ohio as the world's tallest and fastest roller coaster.
- May 9 – Andrew Peacock deposes John Howard as Federal Opposition Leader of Australia.
- May 10 – The government of President of Panama Manuel Noriega declares void the result of the May 7 presidential election, which Noriega had lost to Guillermo Endara.
- May 11
  - · President Bush orders 1,900 U.S. troops to Panama to protect Americans there.
  - The ACT (Australian Capital Territory) Legislative Assembly meets for the first time.
- May 14
  - Mikhail Gorbachev visits China, the first Soviet leader to do so since Nikita Khrushchev in the 1960s.
  - Carlos Menem wins the Argentine presidential election.
- May 15 – Australia's first private tertiary institution, Bond University, opens on the Gold Coast.

- May 16 – Ethiopia Coup Attempt: Senior military officers stage a coup attempt in Ethiopia hours after President Mengistu Haile Mariam leaves on a visit to East Germany.
- May 17 – More than 1 million Chinese protestors march through Beijing demanding greater democracy.
- May 19
  - 1989 Ürümqi unrest: Uyghur and Hui Muslim protesters riot in front of the government building in Ürümqi, China.
  - Tiananmen Square protests of 1989: Zhao Ziyang meets the demonstrators in Tiananmen Square.
  - Ciriaco De Mita resigns as Prime Minister of Italy.
- May 20 – Tiananmen Square protests of 1989: The Chinese government declares martial law in Beijing.
- May 22 – The Nordland Days in Leningrad region (Leningrad Oblast) open.
- May 29
  - Amid food riots and looting set off by inflation, the Government of Argentina declares a nationwide state of siege.
  - Boris Yeltsin gains a seat on the Supreme Soviet of the Soviet Union.
  - Tiananmen Square protests of 1989: The 10 m (33 ft) high *Goddess of Democracy* statue is unveiled in Tiananmen Square by student demonstrators.
  - NATO agrees to talks with the Soviet Union on reducing the number of short-range nuclear weapons in Europe.
  - An attempted assassination of Miguel Maza Marquez, director of the Departamento Administrativo de Seguridad (DAS) in Bogotá, Colombia is committed by members of the Medellín Cartel, who kill 4 and injure 37.
- May 31 – Six members of the guerrilla group Revolutionary Movement Tupac Amaru (MRTA) of Peru, shoot dead 8 transsexuals, in the city of Tarapoto.

June

People's Liberation Army were to drive away students in Tiananmen Square.

- June 1–10 – Pope John Paul II visits Norway, Iceland, Finland, Denmark, and Sweden.
- June 2 – Sōsuke Uno succeeds Noboru Takeshita as Prime Minister of Japan.
- June 3
  - Fighting breaks out in the Uzbek Soviet Socialist Republic between ethnic Uzbeks and the Turkish minority; more than 100 people are killed by June 15.
  - The SkyDome (now known as Rogers Centre) opens in Toronto.
  - The world's first HDTV broadcasts commence in Japan, in analog.
- June 4
  - The Tiananmen Square crackdown takes place in Beijing on the army's approach to the square, and the final stand-off in the square is covered live on television.
  - Solidarity's victory in Polish elections is the first of many anti-communist revolutions in Central and Eastern Europe in 1989.

- Ufa train disaster: A natural gas explosion near Ufa, Russia kills 645 as 2 trains passing each other throw sparks near a leaky pipeline.
- June 5 – An unknown Chinese protestor, "Tank Man", stands in front of a column of military tanks on Chang'an Avenue in Beijing, temporarily halting them, an incident which achieves iconic status internationally through images taken by Western photographers.
- June 6 – The Ayatollah Khomeini's first funeral is aborted by officials after a large crowd storms the funeral procession, nearly destroying Khomeini's wooden coffin in order to get a last glimpse of his body. At one point, Khomeini's body almost falls to the ground, as the crowd attempt to grab pieces of the death shroud.
- June 7 – Surinam Airways Flight 764 crashes in Paramaribo, Suriname; killing 176.
- June 12 – The Corcoran Gallery of Art removes Robert Mapplethorpe's gay photography exhibition.
- June 13 – The wreck of the German battleship *Bismarck*, which was sunk in 1941, is located 600 miles (970 km) west of Brest, France.
- June 15 – In the Irish general election, Fianna Fáil, led by Taoiseach Charles Haughey, fails to win a majority.
- June 16 – A crowd of 250,000 gathers at Heroes Square in Budapest for the historic reburial of Imre Nagy, the former Hungarian prime minister who had been executed in 1958.
- June 18 – In the first Greek legislative election of the year, the Panhellenic Socialist Movement, led by Prime Minister of Greece Andreas Papandreou, loses control of the Hellenic Parliament, leading to Papandreou's resignation on July 2.
- June 21 – British police arrest 250 people for celebrating the summer solstice at Stonehenge.
- June 22 – Ireland's first universities established since independence in 1922, Dublin City University and the University of Limerick, open.
- June 24 – Jiang Zemin becomes General Secretary of the Communist Party of China.

- June 30 – A military coup led by Omar al-Bashir ousts the civilian government of Prime Minister of Sudan Sadiq al-Mahdi.

July

- July 2 – Andreas Papandreou, Prime Minister of Greece resigns; a new government is formed under Tzannis Tzannetakis.
- July 5
  - President of South Africa P. W. Botha meets the imprisoned Nelson Mandela face to face for the first time.
  - The television show *Seinfeld* premieres.
- July 6 – The Tel Aviv–Jerusalem bus 405 suicide attack, the first Palestinian suicide attack on Israel, takes place.
- July 9 – Steffi Graf and Boris Becker of West Germany win singles titles at the 1989 Wimbledon Championships.
- July 9–12 – U.S. President George H. W. Bush travels to Poland and Hungary, pushing for U.S. economic aid and investment.
- July 10
  - Approximately 300,000 Siberian coal miners go on strike, demanding better living conditions and less bureaucracy; it is the largest Soviet labor strike since the 1920s.
  - Mel Blanc, the man of 1000 voices of many characters dies of heart disease aged 81.
- July 12 – In the Republic of Ireland, the Taoiseach Charles Haughey returns to power after Fianna Fáil forms a coalition with the Progressive Democrats.
- July 14 – France celebrates the 200th anniversary of the French Revolution.
- July 14–16 – At the 15th G7 summit, leaders call for restrictions on gas emissions.
- July 17
  - The Northrop Grumman B-2 Spirit Stealth Bomber makes its first flight.
  - Poland and the Vatican re-establish diplomatic relations after approximately 50 years.

- July 18 – Actress Rebecca Schaeffer is murdered by an obsessed fan, leading to stricter stalking laws in California.
- July 19
  - The National Assembly of the Republic of Poland elects Wojciech Jaruzelski to the new and powerful post of President of Poland.
  - United Airlines Flight 232 (Douglas DC-10) crashes in Sioux City, Iowa, killing 112; 184 on board survive.
- July 20 – Burmese opposition leader Aung San Suu Kyi is placed under house arrest. She is released in 2010.
- July 21 – A total blockade of Armenia and NKAO by Azerbaijan begins.
- July 23
  - Japan's ruling Liberal Democratic Party loses control of the House of Councillors, the LDP's worst electoral showing in 34 years, leading to Prime Minister Uno announcing he will resign to take responsibility for the result.
  - Giulio Andreotti takes office as Prime Minister of Italy.
- July 26 – A federal grand jury indicts Cornell University student Robert Tappan Morris for releasing a computer virus, making him the first person to be prosecuted under the 1986 Computer Fraud and Abuse Act.
- July 27 – In what was the largest prison sentence to date, Thai financial scammer Mae Chamoy Thipyaso and her accomplices are each sentenced to 141,078 years in prison.
- July 28 – In the Iranian presidential election, electors overwhelmingly elect Akbar Hashemi Rafsanjani as President of Iran and endorse changes to the Constitution of the Islamic Republic of Iran, increasing the powers of the president.
- July 31
  - In Lebanon, Hezbollah announces that it has hanged U.S. Marine Lt. Col. William R. Higgins in retaliation for Israel's July 28 kidnapping of Hezbollah leader Abdel Karim Obeid. The same day, the United Nations Security Council passes United Nations Security Council Resolution 638,

condemning the taking of hostages by both sides in the conflict.
- ○ Nintendo releases the Game Boy portable video game system in North America.

August

- August 2 – Pakistan is readmitted to the Commonwealth of Nations after leaving it in 1972.
- August 5 – Jaime Paz Zamora is elected President of Bolivia, taking office the next day.
- August 7
  - ○ U.S. Congressman Mickey Leland (D-TX) and 15 others die in a plane crash in Ethiopia.
  - ○ The presidents of five Central American countries agree that the U.S.-backed *contras* fighting the government of Nicaragua should be disbanded and evicted from their bases in Honduras by December 5.
  - ○ Federal Express purchases Flying Tiger Line for approximately 800 million U.S. dollars.
- August 8
  - ○ Prime Minister of New Zealand David Lange resigns for health reasons and is replaced by Geoffrey Palmer.
  - ○ *STS-28*: Space Shuttle *Columbia* takes off on a secret 5-day military mission.
- August 9
  - ○ Toshiki Kaifu becomes Prime Minister of Japan.
  - ○ The asteroid 4769 Castalia is the first asteroid directly imaged by radar from Arecibo Observatory.
  - ○ A measure to rescue the savings and loan industry is signed into law by President Bush, launching the largest federal rescue to date.
- August 10 – Army General Colin Powell became the first black chairman of the Joint Chiefs of Staff after being nominated by President Bush.

- August 13 – A hot air balloon accident near Alice Springs, Australia kills 13.
- August 14
  - P. W. Botha resigns as President of South Africa.
  - The Sega Genesis is released in North America.
- August 15 – F. W. de Klerk becomes the seventh and last State President of apartheid South Africa.
- August 16–17 – The Woodstock '89 Festival takes place.
- August 18 – Leading presidential hopeful Luis Carlos Galán is assassinated near Bogotá in Colombia.
- August 19
  - Polish president Wojciech Jaruzelski nominates Solidarity activist Tadeusz Mazowiecki to be Prime Minister, the first non-communist in power in 42 years.
  - The Pan-European Picnic, a peace demonstration, is held on the Austrian-Hungarian border.
- August 19–21 – In response to the murder of a judge, a provincial police chief, and presidential candidate Galán, the authorities of Colombia arrest 11,000 suspected Colombian drug traffickers.
- August 20
  - In Beverly Hills, California, Lyle and Erik Menendez shoot their wealthy parents to death in the family's den.
  - Fifty-one people die when the Marchioness pleasure boat collides with a barge on the River Thames adjacent to Southwark Bridge.
- August 21 – The 21st anniversary of the crushing of the Prague Spring is commemorated by a demonstration in the city.
- August 23
  - Two million indigenous people of Estonian, Latvian and Lithuanian SSRs join hands to demand freedom and independence from Soviet occupation, forming an uninterrupted 600 km human chain called the Baltic Way.
  - Hungary removes border restrictions with Austria.
  - All of Australia's 1,645 domestic airline pilots resign over an airline's move to sack and sue them over a dispute.

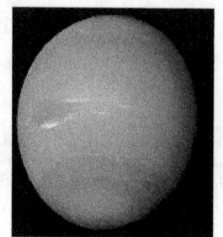

Voyager 2 at Neptune

- August 23 – Yusef Hawkins is shot in the Bensonhurst section of Brooklyn, New York, sparking racial tensions between African Americans and Italian Americans.
- August 24
    - Colombia's cocaine traffickers declare "total and absolute war" against the government and begin a series of bombings and arson attacks.
    - *Voyager 2* makes its closest approach to Neptune.
    - Record-setting baseball player Pete Rose agrees to a lifetime ban from the sport following allegations of illegal gambling, thereby preventing his induction into the Baseball Hall of Fame.
    - Indonesia's first privately owned television station, Rajawali Citra Televisi Indonesia, (RCTI) begins broadcasting.
    - Tadeusz Mazowiecki of Solidarity is elected Prime Minister of Poland.
- August 25 – Voyager 2 passes the planet Neptune and its moon Triton.
- August 31 – In the aftermath of the Chadian–Libyan conflict of 1978–87, representatives of Libya and Chad agree to let the International Court of Justice determine ownership of the Aouzou Strip, which had been occupied by Libya since 1973.

September

- September 6
  - South African general election, 1989, the last held under apartheid, returns the National Party to power with a much-reduced majority.
  - In the Dutch general election, the Christian Democratic Appeal, led by Ruud Lubbers wins 54 seats, and is ultimately able to form a government on November 7 after entering into coalition with the Labour Party.
  - England holds Sweden to a 0–0 draw in Sweden, qualifying for the 1990 FIFA World Cup. The game becomes famous after Terry Butcher sustains a deep cut to his forehead early in the game. He receives stitches but plays on the entire game. By the end of the game, the front of Butcher's white shirt and shorts are almost entirely covered in blood.
- September 7 – Representatives of the government of Ethiopia and Eritrean separatists meet in Atlanta, with former U.S. President Jimmy Carter attempting to broker a peace settlement.
- September 8 – Partnair Flight 394 flies past an F-16 Fighting Falcon on its way home, then the Convair 580 rolls upside down and falls in the North Sea.
- September 10 – The Hungarian government opens the country's western borders to refugees from the German Democratic Republic.
- September 10–11 – Norway's ruling Labour Party loses eight seats in the parliamentary elections, its worst showing since 1945.
- September 14
  - An agreement of cooperation between Leningrad Oblast (Russia) and Nordland County (Norway) is signed in Leningrad, by chairmen Lev Kojkolainen and Sigbjørn Eriksen.
  - Standard Gravure shooting: Joseph T. Wesbecker, a pressman on disability for mental illness, entered his former workplace and killed eight people and injured twelve before committing suicide after a history of suicidal ideation.

- September 17–22 – Hurricane Hugo devastates the Caribbean and the southeastern United States, causing at least 71 deaths and $8 billion in damage.
- September 18 – alleged coup attempt in Burkina Faso foiled.
- September 19
  - The Catholic Church calls for removal of the Carmelite convent located near the former Auschwitz concentration camp, whose presence had offended some Jewish leaders.
  - UTA Flight 772 explodes over Niger, killing all 171 people on board (the Islamic Jihad Organization claims responsibility).
  - Burkinabé ministers Jean-Baptiste Boukary Lingani and Henri Zongo executed following their arrest the previous day.
- September 20 – F. W. de Klerk is sworn in as the seventh and last State President of apartheid South Africa.
- September 22
  - 1989 Deal barracks bombing: An IRA bomb explodes at the Royal Marine School of Music in Deal, Kent, United Kingdom, leaving 11 dead and 22 injured.
  - Doe v. University of Michigan: A Michigan court rules against the hate speech law at the University of Michigan, claiming it unconstitutional.
- September 23 – A cease-fire in the Lebanese Civil War stops the violence that had killed 900 people since March.
- September 26 – Vietnam announces that it has withdrawn the last of its troops from the State of Cambodia, ending an 11-year occupation.
- September 30
  - Nearly 7,000 East Germans who had come to Prague on special refugee trains are allowed to leave for the West.
  - The Senegambia Confederation is dissolved over border disagreements.

October

- October – Cold War – Perestroika – Nathan's Famous opens a hot dog stand in Moscow.
- October 1 – Civil union between partners in a same-sex relationship becomes legal in Denmark under a law enacted on June 7, the world's first such legislation.
- October 3
    - Manuel Noriega, military leader of Panama, foils a plot by junior officers to overthrow him.
    - The government of East Germany closes the country's border with Czechoslovakia to prevent further emigration to the West.
- October 5 – The Dalai Lama wins the Nobel Peace Prize.
- October 6 – Bette Davis, First Lady of American Cinema, dies at 81.
- October 7
    - The communist Hungarian Socialist Workers' Party votes to reorganize itself as a socialist party, to be named the Hungarian Socialist Party.
    - The first mass demonstration against the socialistic regime in the GDR began in Plauen, East Germany, at 7 October 1989 and it was the beginning of a series of mass demonstrations in the whole GDR which ultimately led to the unification of Germany in 1990.
- October 9
    - An official news agency in the Soviet Union reports the landing of a UFO in Voronezh.
    - In Leipzig, East Germany, protesters demand the legalization of opposition groups and democratic reforms.
- October 13
    - Friday the 13th mini-crash: The Dow Jones Industrial Average plunges 190.58 points, or 6.91 percent, to close at 2,569.26, most likely after the junk bond market collapses.

- Gro Harlem Brundtland, leader of the Labour Party, resigns as Prime Minister of Norway. She is succeeded by Jan P. Syse, leader of the Conservative Party, on October 16.
- October 15 – Walter Sisulu is released from prison in South Africa.
- October 17 – The 6.9 Mw Loma Prieta earthquake shakes the San Francisco Bay Area and the Central Coast with a maximum Mercalli intensity of IX (*Violent*). Sixty-three people were killed.
- October 18
  - The Communist leader of East Germany, Erich Honecker, is forced to step down as leader of the country after a series of health problems, and is succeeded by Egon Krenz.
  - The National Assembly of Hungary votes to restore multiparty democracy.
  - NASA launches the unmanned Galileo orbiter on a mission to study the planet Jupiter.

The Phillips Disaster

- October 19
  - The Guildford Four are freed after 14 years.
  - The Wonders of Life pavilion opens at Epcot in Walt Disney World, Florida.
- October 21 – The Heads of Government of the Commonwealth of Nations issue the Langkawi Declaration on the Environment, making environmental sustainability one of the Commonwealth's main priorities.
- October 23
  - The Hungarian Republic is officially declared by president Mátyás Szűrös (replacing the Hungarian People's Republic), exactly 33 years after the Hungarian Revolution of 1956.

- The Phillips Disaster in Pasadena, Texas kills 23 and injures 314 others.
- October 31
  - The Grand National Assembly of Turkey elects Prime Minister Turgut Özal as the eighth President of Turkey.
  - Half a million people demonstrate in the East German city of Leipzig.

November

Germans standing on top of the Berlin Wall

- November – First commercial dial-up Internet connection in North America is made, by The World STD.
- November – The first Walmart store in the Northeastern United States, a Sam's Club, is opened in Delran, New Jersey.
- November – Construction of the Denver Airport commences.
- November 1
  - The President of Nicaragua ends a cease-fire with U.S.-backed *contras* that had been in effect since April 1988.
  - The border between East Germany and Czechoslovakia is reopened.
- November 2 – North Dakota and South Dakota celebrate their 100th birthdays.
- November 3 – East German refugees arrive at the West German town of Hof after being allowed through Czechoslovakia.
- November 4 – Typhoon Gay devastates Thailand's Chumphon Province.
- November 6 – The Asia-Pacific Economic Cooperation (APEC) is founded.

- November 7
  - Douglas Wilder wins the Virginia governor's race, becoming the first elected African American governor in the United States.
  - David Dinkins becomes the first African American mayor of New York City.
  - Cold War: The Communist government of East Germany resigns, although SED leader Egon Krenz remains head of state.
- November 9
  - Cold War and Fall of the Berlin Wall: Günter Schabowski accidentally states in a live broadcast press conference that new rules for traveling from East Germany to West Germany will be put in effect "immediately". East Germany opens checkpoints in the Berlin Wall, allowing its citizens to travel freely to West Germany for the first time in decades (November 17 celebrates Germans tearing the wall down).
  - Yıldırım Akbulut of ANAP forms the new government of Turkey (47th government).
- November 10
  - After 45 years of Communist rule in Bulgaria, Bulgarian Communist Party leader Todor Zhivkov is replaced by Foreign Minister Petar Mladenov, who changes the party's name to the Bulgarian Socialist Party.
  - Gaby Kennard becomes the first Australian woman to fly solo around the world.
  - CKO (a Canadian national all-news radio network) suddenly terminates all broadcasting during the newscast at noon (Eastern time), due to financial losses (the station began broadcasting on July 1, 1977).
- November 11 – Louie Espinoza is inaugurated as WBO World Featherweight Champion.
- November 12 – Brazil holds its first free presidential election since 1960. This marks the first time that all Ibero-American nations, excepting Cuba, have elected constitutional governments simultaneously.

- November 13 – Hans-Adam II becomes Prince of Liechtenstein on the death of his father, Prince Franz Joseph II.
- November 14 – Elections are held in Namibia, leading to a victory for the South West Africa People's Organisation.
- November 15
  - Lech Wałęsa, leader of Poland's Solidarity movement, addresses a Joint session of the United States Congress.
  - Brazil holds the first round of its first free election in 29 years; Fernando Collor de Mello and Luiz Inácio Lula da Silva are qualified to the second round, which will be disputed the following month.
- November 16
  - Six Jesuit priests—among them Ignacio Ellacuría, Segundo Montes, and Ignacio Martín-Baró—their housekeeper, and her teenage daughter, are murdered by U.S. trained Salvadoran soldiers (for more information see Murder of UCA scholars).
  - The first American cosmetics shop, an Estée Lauder outlet, opens in Moscow.
  - South African President F. W. de Klerk announces the scrapping of the Separate Amenities Act.
  - UNESCO adopts the Seville Statement on Violence at the 25th session of its General Conference.

A peaceful demonstration in Prague during the Velvet Revolution.

- November 17
  - Cold War – Velvet Revolution: A peaceful student demonstration in Prague, Czechoslovakia, is severely beaten back by riot police. This sparks a revolution aimed at

overthrowing the Communist government (it succeeds on December 29).
- o Disney's *The Little Mermaid* premieres in selected theaters.
- November 20 – Cold War – Velvet Revolution: The number of peaceful protesters assembled in Prague, Czechoslovakia, swells from 200,000 the day before to an estimated half-million.
- November 21 – The Members of the Constituent Assembly of Namibia begin to draft the Constitution of Namibia, which will be the constitution of the newly independent Namibia.
- November 22 – In West Beirut, a bomb explodes near the motorcade of Lebanese President René Moawad and kills him.
- November 24 – Following a week of demonstrations demanding free elections and other reforms, General Secretary Miloš Jakeš and other leaders of the Communist Party of Czechoslovakia resign. Jakeš is replaced by Karel Urbánek.
- November 26
  - o The Saskatchewan Roughriders win on a last seconds field goal to win a major points output; winning the 77th Grey Cup versus the Hamilton Tiger-Cats 43-40.
  - o Uruguayan general election, 1989: Luis Alberto Lacalle is elected President of Uruguay.
- November 28 – Cold War – Velvet Revolution: The Communist Party of Czechoslovakia announces they will give up their monopoly on political power (elections held in December bring the first non-communist government to Czechoslovakia in more than 40 years).
- November 29 – Rajiv Gandhi resigns as Prime Minister of India after his party, the Indian National Congress, loses about half of its seats in the Indian general election.
- November 30 – Deutsche Bank board member Alfred Herrhausen is killed by a bomb (the Red Army Faction claims responsibility for the murder).

December

- December 1
  - In a meeting with Pope John Paul II, President of the Soviet Union Mikhail Gorbachev pledges greater religious freedom for citizens of the Soviet Union.
  - Cold War: East Germany's parliament abolishes the constitutional provision granting the Communist-dominated SED its monopoly on power. Egon Krenz, the Politburo and the Central Committee resign 2 days later.
  - A military coup attempt begins in the Philippines against the government of Philippine President Corazon C. Aquino. It is crushed by United States intervention ending by December 9.
- December 2
  - The *Solar Maximum Mission* scientific research satellite, launched in 1980, crashes back to earth.
  - V. P. Singh takes office as Prime Minister of India.
  - In the Republic of China legislative election, the Kuomintang suffers its worst election setback in 40 years in power, winning only 53% of the popular vote.
  - The Second Malayan Emergency concludes with a peace agreement. The Malayan Communist Party disbands and Chin Peng remains in exile in Thailand until his death in 2013.
  - The last two Japanese World War II holdout troops surrender.
- December 3
  - The entire leadership of the ruling Socialist Unity Party in East Germany, including Egon Krenz, resigns.
  - Cold War: Malta Summit – In a meeting off the coast of Malta, U.S. President George H. W. Bush and Soviet leader Mikhail Gorbachev release statements indicating that the Cold War between their nations may be coming to an end.
- December 4 – Prime Minister of Jordan Zaid ibn Shaker resigns and is replaced by Mudar Badran.
-

- December 6
  - The DAS Building bombing occurs in Bogotá, killing at least 100 people.
  - Egon Krenz resigns as Chairman of the State Council of the German Democratic Republic, and is replaced by Manfred Gerlach, the first non-Communist to hold that post.
  - École Polytechnique massacre (or Montreal Massacre): Marc Lépine, an anti-feminist gunman, murders 14 young women at the École Polytechnique de Montréal.
  - The last episode of the classic era of *Doctor Who* is broadcast on British television.
- December 7
  - Ladislav Adamec resigns as Prime Minister of Czechoslovakia. He is succeeded by Marián Čalfa on December 10.
  - The Lithuanian Soviet Socialist Republic becomes the first of the republics of the Soviet Union to abolish the Communist Party's monopoly on power.
- December 9 – The Socialist Unity Party of Germany elects the reformist Gregor Gysi as party leader.
- December 10
  - President of Czechoslovakia Gustáv Husák swears in a new cabinet with a non-Communist and then immediately resigns as president.
  - Tsakhiagiin Elbegdorj announces the establishment of Mongolia's democratic movement, that peacefully changes the second oldest communist country into a democratic society.
- December 11 – The International Trans-Antarctica Expedition, a group of six explorers from six nations, reaches the South Pole.
- December 14 – Chile holds its first free election in 16 years, electing Patricio Aylwin as president.
- December 15 – Drug baron José Gonzalo Rodríguez Gacha is killed by Colombian police.

Protests in Romania, December 1989.

- December 17
  - The Romanian Revolution begins in Timișoara when rioters break into the building housing the District Committee of the Romanian Communist Party and cause extensive damage. Their attempts to set the buildings on fire are foiled by military units.
  - Brazil holds the second round of its first free election in 29 years; Fernando Collor de Mello is elected to serve as President from 1990.
  - The first full-length episode of the animated series *The Simpsons*, "Simpsons Roasting on an Open Fire", is shown on Fox television in the United States.

Flames engulf a building following the United States invasion of Panama.

- December 19 – Workers in Romanian cities go on strike in protest against the communist regime.
- December 20 – The United States invasion of Panama ("Operation Just Cause") is launched in an attempt to overthrow Panamanian dictator Manuel Noriega.
- December 21 – Nicolae Ceaușescu addresses an assembly of some 110,000 people outside the Romanian Communist Party

headquarters in Bucharest. The crowd begin to protest against Ceaușescu and he orders the army to attack the protesters.

- December 22
  - After a week of bloody demonstrations, Ion Iliescu takes over as president of Romania, ending the communist dictatorship of Nicolae Ceaușescu, who flees his palace in a helicopter to escape inevitable execution after the palace is invaded by rioters. The Romanian troops, who the day before had followed Ceaușescu's orders to attack the demonstrators, change sides and join the uprising.
  - Two tourist coaches collide on the Pacific highway north of Kempsey, Australia, killing 35.
- December 23 – Nicolae and Elena Ceaușescu are captured in Târgoviște.
- December 25
  - Romanian leader Nicolae Ceaușescu and his wife Elena are executed by military troops after being found guilty of crimes against humanity.
  - Bank of Japan governors announce a major interest rate hike, eventually leading to the peak and fall of the *bubble economy*.
- December 28 – A magnitude 5.6 earthquake hits Newcastle, New South Wales, Australia, killing 13 people.
- December 29
  - Václav Havel is elected president of Czechoslovakia.
  - Riots break out after Hong Kong decides to forcibly repatriate Vietnamese refugees.
  - Nikkei 225 for Tokyo Stock Exchange hits its all-time intra-day high of 38,957.44 and closing high at 38,915.87.
  - Spümcø, the company that produces *Ren and Stimpy*, is incorporated in California.
- December 31 – Poland's president signs the Balcerowicz Plan, ending the state socialist system in Poland in favor of a capitalist system and Polish involvement in the Warsaw Pact.

Date unknown

- The first Al-Qaeda-related cell in the United States begins operation in New York City.
- Alan Bond's Bond Corporation goes into receivership with the largest debt in Australian history.
- The United States leaves its embassy in Kabul, Afghanistan, it does not return until late 2001.
- Homosexual acts between consenting adults are decriminalized in Western Australia.
- Kamchatka opens to Russian civilian visitors.
- The Breguet Alizé propeller-driven anti-submarine planes are retired from active carrier service in the French Navy.
- The first national park in the Netherlands is established in Schiermonnikoog.
- Ebenezer Floppen Slopper's Wonderful Water slides in Oakbrook Terrace, Illinois closes after an incident on one of the slides.
- Soviet submarine K-173 (*Chelyabinsk*) is commissioned.
- The wreck of the *Lady Elgin* is discovered off Highland Park, Illinois by Harry Zych.
- Richard C. Duncan introduces the Olduvai theory, about the collapse of industrial civilization.
- The NIOS board is established by the Ministry of Human Resource Development of the Government of India.
- The Museum of Jurassic Technology is founded in Culver City, California, by David and Diana Wilson.
- The last Golden toad is seen; the species is now classified extinct.
- The Japan Fantasy Novel Award is established.
- The global concentration of carbon dioxide in Earth's atmosphere reaches 350 parts per million by volume.
- Walmart posts revenues and profits triple its 1986 figures and rivals Kmart and Sears in importance in the American market.
- N.W.A are the first gangsta rap group to sell a million copies of an album; their album *Straight Outta Compton*.
- The South African military dismantles its last nuclear weapons.

Births

January

Nina Dobrev

Yasmien Kurdi

Emily Hughes

Khleo Thomas

- January 1
  - Adèle Haenel, French actress
  - Edita Vilkevičiūtė, Lithuanian model
- January 2 – Kaitlin Howell, Canadian actress
- January 3
  - Alex D. Linz, American actor
  - Anya Kop, American fashion model
  - Kōhei Uchimura, Japanese gymnast
- January 4
  - Kariem Hussein, Swiss 400 metres hurdler
  - Sessilee Lopez, American model
  - Julius Yego, Kenian javelin thrower
- January 6
  - Andy Carroll, English footballer
  - James Durbin, American Idol contestant
  - Nicky Romero, Dutch DJ
- January 7 – Emiliano Insúa, Argentine footballer
- January 9
  - Michael Beasley, American basketball player
  - Nina Dobrev, Bulgarian-Canadian actress
- January 10 – Emily Meade, American film and television actress
- January 11
  - Chris Perry-Metcalf, British actor
  - Naif Hazazi, Saudi footballer
- January 12 – Arci Muñoz, Filipina actress & model
- January 14 – Frankie Sandford, British singer

- January 15
  - Alexei Cherepanov, Russian ice hockey player (d. 2008)
  - Keiffer Hubbell, American ice dancer
  - Tasha Reign, American pornographic actress, nude model, stripper, producer and sex columnist
  - Ronny Vencatachellum, Mauritian swimmer
- January 16 – Yvonne Zima, American actress
- January 19 – Yani Tseng, Taiwanese golfer
- January 20 – Nadia Di Cello, Argentine actress
- January 21
  - Katie Griffiths, English actress
  - Doğuş Balbay, American basketball player
  - Sergey Fesikov, Russian swimmer
  - Henrikh Mkhitaryan, Armenian footballer
- January 22 – Jared Smith, American singer
- January 24
  - Calvin Goldspink, British actor
  - Gong Lijiao, Chinese shot putter
- January 25
  - Mikako Tabe, Japanese stage and film actress
  - Yasmien Kurdi, Filipino actress and singer
- January 26 – Emily Hughes, American figure skater
- January 27
  - Ricky van Wolfswinkel, Dutch footballer
  - Daisy Lowe, English fashion model
- January 30
  - Khleo Thomas, American actor and rapper
  - Jahvid Best, American NFL player

February

Jeremy Sumpter

Cristine Reyes

Elizabeth Olsen

- February 3 – Ryne Sanborn, American actor
- February 4 – Larissa Ramos, Brazilian Miss Earth 2009 winner

- February 5
  - Jeremy Sumpter, American actor
  - Cristine Reyes, Filipina actress
- February 7
  - Louisa Lytton, English actress
  - Neil Taylor, Welsh footballer
  - Isaiah Thomas, American basketball player

Corbin Bleu

Scout Taylor-Compton

- February 8 – Danielle Harmer, English actress
- February 9 – Wu Chia-ching, Taiwanese pool player
- February 11
  - Elisa Izquierdo, American murder victim (d. 1995)
  - Lovi Poe, Filipina actress
- February 13
  - Rodrigo Possebon, Brazilian footballer
  - Carly McKillip, Canadian actress

- February 16
    - Elizabeth Olsen, American actress
    - Zivanna Letisha Siregar, Indonesian model
- February 17
    - Chord Overstreet, American actor, singer and musician
    - Rebecca Adlington, British swimmer
- February 21
    - Corbin Bleu, American actor and singer
    - Kristin Herrera, American actress
    - Scout Taylor-Compton, American actress
- February 23 – Chris Conte, American NFL player
- February 24
    - Kosta Koufos, Greek-American basketball player
    - Trace Cyrus, American musician
- February 25 – Lee Sang-hwa, South Korean speed skater
- February 26 – Anastassiya Bannova, Kazakh archer
- February 27
    - Kelly Breeding, American singer
    - Stephen Kiprotich, Ugandan marathoner
    - Stefano Langone, American singer
    - Lloyd Rigby, English footballer
- February 28 – Zhang Liyin, Chinese singer

March

Daniella Monet

Anton Yelchin

Takeru Satoh

Alyson Michalka

- March 1
  - Tenille Dashwood, Australian professional wrestler
  - Daniella Monet, American actress
  - Carlos Vela, Mexican footballer

- March 4 – Erin Heatherton, American fashion model
- March 5
  - Sterling Knight, American actor
  - Jake Lloyd, American actor
- March 6 – Agnieszka Radwańska, Polish tennis player
- March 7 – Gerald Anderson, Filipino-American actor
- March 9 – Kim Tae-yeon, South Korean singer (Girls' Generation)
- March 11
  - Daniella Kertesz, Israeli actress
  - Anton Yelchin, Russian-born American actor (d. 2016)
- March 14 – Colby O'Donis, American singer
- March 15 – Caitlin Wachs, American actress
- March 16
  - Peaches Geldof, British performer (d. 2014)
  - Blake Griffin, American basketball player
  - Theo Walcott, English footballer
- March 17
  - Mason Musso, American singer
  - Shinji Kagawa, Japanese football player
- March 18
  - Francesco Checcucci, Italian footballer
  - Lily Collins, English-American actress
  - Kana Nishino, Japanese singer-songwriter
- March 20 – Fei Fei Sun, Chinese model
- March 21
  - Rochelle Wiseman, British singer (S Club Juniors & The Saturdays)
  - Labrinth, English singer-songwriter and record producer
  - Takeru Satoh, Japanese actor (Rurouni Kenshin)
- March 22
  - Eva Pereira, Cape Verdean middle distance runner
  - Karen Rodriguez, American singer
  - J. J. Watt, American football player
  - Aline Weber, Brazilian model
- March 24 – Aziz Shavershian, Australian bodybuilder (d. 2011)
-

- March 25
  - Scott Sinclair, English footballer
  - Alyson Michalka, American actress and singer
- March 29 – Arnold Peralta, Honduran footballer (d. 2015)
- March 31 – Liu Zige, Chinese swimmer

April

Aysel Teymurzadeh

- April 2 – Ankit Narang, Indian actor
- April 2 – Midhun Jith, Martial artist, Guinness World Records breaker & World Kickboxing Champion
- April 4 – Chris Herd, Australian footballer who currently plays for Premier League team Aston Villa
- April 8
  - Nicholas Megalis, American singer-songwriter
  - Hitomi Takahashi, Japanese singer
- April 17 – Javed Mohammed, Trinidadian footballer
- April 18
  - Jessica Jung, Korean American singer (SNSD)
  - Alia Shawkat, American actress
- April 22
  - Catherine Banner, British author
  - Thomas James Longley, British actor
  - Louis Smith, British gymnast
  -

- April 23
  - Anastasia Baranova, Russian-born actress
  - Nicole Vaidišová, Czech tennis player
- April 25
  - Raquel Donatelli, American reality television star
  - Emanuela de Paula, Brazilian model
  - Michael van Gerwen, Dutch darts player
  - Aysel Teymurzadeh, Azerbaijani pop and R&B singer
- April 26 – Daesung, South Korean singer
- April 27
  - Lars Bender, German footballer
  - Sven Bender, German footballer
  - Martha Hunt, American model
- April 28 – Kim Sung-kyu, South Korean singer and dancer (Infinite)
- April 29 – Foxes, British singer-songwriter.

May

Katinka Hosszú

- May 3 – Katinka Hosszú, Hungarian swimmer
- May 4
  - Dániel Gyurta, Hungarian swimmer
  - Rory McIlroy, Northern Irish golfer
  - James van Riemsdyk, American ice hockey player
- May 5 – Chris Brown, American singer and actor
-

- May 6
  - Dominika Cibulková, Slovak tennis player
  - Otto Knows, Swedish DJ and producer
- May 7
  - Arlenis Sosa, Dominican model
  - Earl Thomas, American football player
- May 8 – Katy B, British singer
- May 10 – Lindsey Shaw, American actress
- May 11
  - Cam Newton, American football player, Quarterback and #1 on the Carolina Panthers
  - Giovani dos Santos, Mexican footballer
- May 12
  - Eleftheria Eleftheriou, Greek-Cypriot singer and actress
  - Imogen Poots, English actress
- May 14
  - Melinda Bam, South African beauty pageant contestant and model
  - Rob Gronkowski, American football player
  - Alina Talay, Belarusian 100 metres hurdler
- May 15 – Sunny Lee, Korean-American singer (SNSD)
- May 16 – Behati Prinsloo, Namibian fashion model
- May 17 – Tessa Virtue, Canadian ice dancer
- May 18 – Shreevats Goswami, Indian cricketer
- May 19 – Gaelan Connell, American actor and musician
- May 21 – Hal Robson-Kanu, Welsh footballer
- May 23
  - Patrick Hougaard, Danish motorcycle speedway rider
  - Ezequiel Schelotto, Italian football player
- May 24 – G-Eazy, Rapper and producer
- May 25
  - Guillaume Boivin, Canadian racing cyclist
  - Aliona Moon, Moldovan singer
- May 27
  - Afgan Syahreza, Indonesian pop singer and actor
  -

- May 29
  - Eyþór Ingi Gunnlaugsson, Icelandic singer
  - Riley Keough, American model
  - Brandon Mychal Smith, American actor
- May 30 – Park Hyomin, South Korean singer
- May 31
  - Pablo Alborán, Spanish singer
  - Bas Dost, Dutch football player
  - Sean Johnson, American football player
  - Daul Kim, South Korean model (d. 2009)
  - Marco Reus, German football player
  - Chase Stanley, Australian rugby player
  - Sean Thornley, British tennis player

June

Willy Moon

- June 2
  - Freddy Adu, American soccer player
  - Cooper Helfet, American football player
  - Willy Moon, New Zealand singer
- June 3 – Jillette Johnson, American singer
- June 4
  - Pawel Fajdek, Polish hammer thrower
  - Eldar Gasimov, Azerbaijani singer
- June 5
  - Cam Atkinson, American ice hockey player
  - Monica Castaño, Colombian beauty queen and model

Lucy Hale

- June 8
  - Richard Fleeshman, English actor
  - Amaury Vassili, French opera singer and professional tenor
- June 9 – Chloë Agnew, Irish singer
- June 10 – Alexandra Stan, Romanian singer

Christopher Mintz-Plasse

- June 12 – Krista Kleiner, Filipina-American beauty queen, singer, model, actress and martial artist
  - Trenton Smith, American writer
- June 13
  - Tommy Searle, British Motocross Racer
  - Lisa Tucker, American singer, musical theater and television actress
- June 14 – Lucy Hale, American actress and singer
- June 17 – Simone Battle, American actress and singer (d. 2014)
- June 18
  - Anna Fenninger, Austrian alpine ski racer

- o Renee Olstead, American actress and singer
- June 20 – Christopher Mintz-Plasse, American actor
- June 22 – Jeffrey Earnhardt, American race car driver
- June 23 – Lauren Bennett, British singer, dancer, painter, photographer, and model

Matthew Lewis

- June 27
  - o Matthew Lewis, British actor
  - o Bruna Tenório, Brazilian supermodel
- June 28
  - o Mark Fischbach, American YouTube personality
  - o Joe Kovacs, American shot putter
- June 30 – Ginta Lapiņa, Latvian model

July

David Henrie

Daniel Radcliffe

Victoria Azarenka

- July 1 Daniel Ricciardo, Formula 1 driver. Drives for Red Bull F1
- July 2 – Devin Tailes, American singer
- July 3 – Elle King, American singer, songwriter and actress
- July 8
  - Dmitry Abakumov, Russian football player
  - Yarden Gerbi, Israeli world champion judoka
- July 11
  - David Henrie, American actor
  - Shareeka Epps, American actress
- July 12
  - Phoebe Tonkin, Australian actress
- July 13 – Sayumi Michishige, Japanese singer
- July 14
  - Cyril Rioli, Australian rules footballer
  - Sean Flynn-Amir, American actor
- July 15 – Tristan Wilds, American actor and singer
- July 16
  - Gareth Bale, Welsh footballer

- o Carlito Olivero, American singer
- July 18
  - o Yohan Mollo, French footballer
  - o Jamie Benn, Canadian ice hockey player
- July 21
  - o Narcissa Wright, speedrunner
  - o Rory Culkin, American actor
  - o Jamie Waylett, British actor
  - o Juno Temple, British actress
- July 22
  - o Keegan Allen, American actor
  - o Baltasar Breki Samper, Icelandic actor
- July 23
  - o Daniel Radcliffe, British actor
  - o KJ Wright, American football player
  - o Zhong An Qi, Taiwanese singer
- July 25 – Noel Callahan, Canadian actor
- July 27 – Charlotte Arnold, Canadian actress
- July 28
  - o Felipe Kitadai, Brazilian Olympic medalist judoka
  - o Amy Yang, South Korean golfer
- July 30 – Aleix Espargaró, Spanish Grand prix motorcycle racer
- July 31
  - o Alexis Knapp, American actress and singer
  - o Marshall Williams, Canadian actor
  - o Jessica Williams, American actress
  - o Victoria Azarenka, Belarusian tennis player

August

Jessica Mauboy

Joe Jonas and Carlos Pena Jr. born August 15

Hayden Panettiere

Juliana Cannarozzo

- August 1
  - Tiffany Hwang, Korean-American singer (SNSD)
  - Madison Bumgarner, American baseball player
  - Tomoka Kurokawa, Japanese actress
- August 2
  - Nacer Chadli, Belgian footballer
  - Vanes-Mari Du Toit, South African netball player
- August 3
  - Jules Bianchi, French Formula One driver (d. 2015)
  - Sam Hutchinson, English footballer
- August 4
  - Jessica Mauboy, Australian singer-songwriter and actress (Young Divas)
  - Wang Hao, Chinese chess player
- August 5
  - Nina Radojčić, Serbian singer
  - Mathieu Manset, French footballer
  - Jessica Nigri, American model and actress
  - Shanshan Feng, Chinese golfer
- August 7
  - DeMar DeRozan, American basketball player
- August 8
  - Ken Baumann, American actor and author
  - Sesil Karatantcheva, Bulgarian tennis player
  - Anthony Rizzo, American baseball player
  - Hannah Miley, English-Scottish swimmer

- o Aleksandra Szwed, Polish actress and singer
- August 9
  - o Stefano Okaka, Italian footballer
  - o Lucy Dixon, English actress
  - o Meredith Deane, American actress
  - o Jason Heyward, American baseball player
- August 10
  - o Ben Sahar, Israeli footballer
  - o Sam Gagner, Canadian ice hockey player
  - o Brenton Thwaites, Australian actor
- August 11
  - o Gui Gui, Taiwanese singer and actress (Hey Girl)
  - o Junior Heffernan, Irish cyclist and triathlete (d. 2013)
  - o Sebastian Huke, German footballer
- August 14 – Kyle Turris, Canadian ice hockey player
- August 15
  - o Belinda, Mexican singer and actress
  - o Joe Jonas, American musician, actor, and singer
  - o Carlos Pena Jr., American actor, dancer and singer
- August 19 – Romeo Miller, American rapper and actor
- August 20 – Kirko Bangz, American rapper
- August 21 – Hayden Panettiere, American actress and singer
- August 23 – Breanna Conrad, American reality television star
- August 26 – James Harden, American basketball player
- August 27 – Juliana Cannarozzo, American figure skater
- August 28
  - o Cassadee Pope, American singer-songwriter
  - o Valtteri Bottas, Formula One driver

September

Avicii

Logan Henderson

Steliana Nistor

Pia Wurtzbach

- September 1
  - Bill Kaulitz, German singer (Tokio Hotel)
  - Jefferson Montero, Ecuadorian footballer
  - Daniel Sturridge, English footballer
- September 2
  - Alexandre Pato, Brazilian footballer
- September 5
  - Kat Graham, Swiss-born, American actress, model, singer and dancer.
- September 7 – Hugh Mitchell, British actor
- September 8 – Avicii, Swedish DJ, remixer, and record producer
  - Sebastián Francini, Argentine actor.
- September 9 – Sean Malto, American Professional Skateboarder
- September 12
  - Freddie Freeman, American baseball player
  - Andrew Luck, American football player
- September 13
  - Jon Mannah, Australian rugby league player (d. 2013)
  - Thomas Müller, German football player

- September 14 – Logan Henderson, Lebanese American actor, dancer, and singer
- September 15 – Steliana Nistor, Romanian gymnast and Olympic medalist
- September 19 – Tyreke Evans, American basketball player, 2010 NBA Rookie of the Year
- September 21 – Jason Derulo, American singer-songwriter, actor
- September 22
  - Hyoyeon Kim, South Korean singer (SNSD)
  - Sabine Lisicki, German tennis player
- September 23
  - Brandon Jennings, American basketball player
  - Kevin Norwood, American football player
  - Sui He, Chinese model
- September 24 – Pia Wurtzbach, German-Filipina actress, model, and Miss Universe 2015 beauty pageant titleholder
- September 26
  - Emma Rigby, British actress
  - Kieran Gibbs, English footballer
- September 27 – Park Tae-hwan, South Korean swimmer
- September 29 – Theo Adams, British performance artist

October

Brie Larson

Mia Wasikowska

Nastia Liukin

- October 1 – Brie Larson, American actress
- October 4
  - Dakota Johnson, American actress
  - Lil Mama, American rapper
  - Kimmie Meissner, American figure skater
  - Viktoria Rebensburg, German alpine skier
  - Rich Homie Quan, American rapper
- October 10 – Aimee Teegarden, American actress
- October 11 – Michelle Wie, American golf player
- October 12 – Paulo Henrique Ganso, Brazilian football player
- October 13 – Skyler Page, American animator and voice actor
- October 14 – Mia Wasikowska, Australian actress
- October 16
  - Dan Biggar, Welsh rugby union player
  - Jack Salvatore, Jr., American actor
- October 19 – Janine Tugonon, Filipina beauty queen
- October 20 – Jess Glynne, British singer

- October 24
  - Armin Bačinović, Slovenian football midfielder
  - T'erea Brown, American track and field athlete
  - Jack Colback, English footballer
  - B. J. Daniels, American football quarterback
  - Cristian Gamboa, Costa Rican footballer
  - Shenae Grimes, Canadian actress
  - Eric Hosmer, American professional baseball player
  - Felix Kjellberg, Swedish YouTube celebrity
  - Igor Pisanjuk, footballer
  - Eliza Taylor, Australian actress
- October 25 – Marina Keegan, American author and journalist
- October 30 – Nastia Liukin, American gymnast and Olympic gold medalist

November

Candice Glover

- November 2 – Katelyn Tarver, American singer, songwriter, actress
- November 3
  - Paula DeAnda, Mexican-American singer
  - Kim Taek-yong, South Korean professional gamer (StarCraft, Starcraft II)
  - Elliott Tittensor, English actor
  - Luke Tittensor, English actor

- November 5 – Andrew Boyce, English footballer
- November 6 – Jozy Altidore, American soccer player
- November 8 – Giancarlo Stanton, American baseball player
- November 9 – Gianluca Bezzina, Maltese doctor, singer
- November 10 – Taron Egerton, English actor
- November 11 – Reina Tanaka, Japanese singer
- November 14 – Jake Livermore, English footballer
- November 19 – Tyga, American rapper
- November 20 – Cody Linley, American actor
- November 22 – Candice Glover, *American Idol* Season 12 winner
- November 24
    - Adam George, British musician
    - Jordan Witzigreuter, American singer/songwriter (The Ready Set)
- November 25 – Tom Dice, Belgian singer-songwriter
- November 27
    - Freddie Sears, English footballer
    - Loveli, Japanese model

December

Nicholas Hoult

Taylor Swift

Ashley Benson

- December 2
    - Cassie Steele, Canadian actress and singer
    - Robert Turbin, American football player
- December 3 – Bette Franke, Dutch model
- December 4 – Garron DuPree, American musician
- December 5
    - Katy Kung, Hong Kong actress
    - Kwon Yuri, South Korean singer (SNSD)
    - Gregory Tyree Boyce, American actor
- December 9 – Eric Bledsoe, American basketball player
- December 10 – Marion Maréchal-Le Pen, French politician
- December 11 – Sam Pinto, Filipina actress and commercial model
- December 12 – Janelle Arthur, American Idol contestant
- December 13
    - Taylor Swift, American singer-songwriter
    - Katherine Schwarzenegger, American author
- December 14 – Onew, Korean singer (SHINee)
- December 18 – Ashley Benson, American actress
- December 19 – Valdimar Bergstað, Icelandic horse rider
- December 21 – Tamannaah, Indian model and actress
- December 22 – Jordin Sparks, American singer
- December 26 – Yohan Blake, Jamaican athlete
- December 27 – Kateryna Lagno, Ukrainian chess player
- December 28
    - Mackenzie Rosman, American actress
    - Jessie Buckley, Irish actress and singer
- December 29
    - Jane Levy, American actress

- o Kei Nishikori, Japanese tennis player
- o Left Brain, American rapper and music producer (Odd Future)
- December 30 – Ryan Sheckler, American skateboarder

Deaths

January

Hirohito

José Luis Bustamante y Rivero

Salvador Dalí

Ted Bundy

- January 3 – Robert Banks, American chemist (b. 1921)
- January 4 – Dvora Netzer, Israeli politician (b. 1897)
- January 7
  - Frank Adams, British mathematician (b. 1930)
  - Hirohito, Emperor of Japan (b. 1901)
- January 8 – Kenneth McMillan, American actor (b. 1932)
- January 10
  - Hai Deng, abbot of Shaolin Temple (b. 1902?)
  - Herbert Morrison, American radio reporter (b. 1905)
  - Donald Voorhees, American composer and musician (b. 1903)
- January 11
  - August Koern, Estonian statesman and diplomat (b. 1900)
  - José Bustamante y Rivero, Peruvian politician, diplomat and jurist, former President (b. 1894)
- January 13 – Joe Spinell, American actor (Maniac, The Last Horror Film) (b. 1936)
- January 14
  - Robert B. Anderson, American administrator and businessman (b. 1910)
  - Robert Lembke, German television presenter and game show host (b. 1913)
- January 16
  - Prem Nazir, Indian actor (b. 1926)
  - Trey Wilson, American actor (b. 1948)
- January 18 – Bruce Chatwin, British author (b. 1940)
- January 19 – Norma Varden, English actress (b. 1898)

- January 20
  - Beatrice Lillie, Canadian actress (b. 1894)
  - Józef Cyrankiewicz, Polish statesman, former Prime Minister and head of State (b. 1911)
- January 21
  - Carl Furillo, American baseball player (b. 1922)
  - Billy Tipton, American musician (b. 1914)
- January 23 – Salvador Dalí, Spanish artist (b. 1904)
- January 24 – Ted Bundy, American serial killer (executed) (b. 1946)
- January 27
  - Bayani Casimiro, Filipino dancer and actor (b. 1918)
  - Thomas Sopwith, English aviation pioneer and yachtsman (b. 1888)

February

Osamu Tezuka

Konrad Lorenz

- February 1 – Elaine de Kooning, American artist (b. 1919)
- February 2 – Ondrej Nepela, Slovakian figure skater (b. 1951)
- February 3
  - John Cassavetes, American actor and author (b. 1929)
  - Glenna Collett-Vare, American golfer (b. 1903)

- February 5 – Joe Morrison, University of South Carolina Head Football Coach (b. 1937)
- February 6
  - Barbara Tuchman, American historian (b. 1912)
  - Netty Herawaty, Indonesian actress (b. 1930)
  - Ron Field, American choreographer (b. 1934)
- February 8 – Lael Rodrigues, Brazilian filmmaker (b. 1951)
- February 9 – Osamu Tezuka, Japanese manga artist, e.g. *Astro Boy* (b. 1928)
- February 11
  - Shakhbut bin Sultan Al Nahyan, Sheikh, former ruler of Abu Dhabi (b. 1905)
  - T. E. B. Clarke, English screenwriter (b. 1907)
  - George O'Hanlon, American actor and director (b. 1912)
- February 14 – Vincent Crane, British musician (Atomic Rooster) (b. 1943)
- February 17
  - Lefty Gomez, Mexican-American baseball player (New York Yankees) and member of the MLB Hall of Fame (b. 1908)
  - Joe Raposo, musician, composer for *Sesame Street* and *The Electric Company* (b. 1937)
- February 20 – Robert Dorning, English actor (b. 1913)
- February 21 – Moshe Unna, Israeli politician (b. 1902)
- February 24 – Sparky Adams, American baseball player (b. 1894)
- February 26 – Roy Eldridge, American musician (b. 1911)
- February 27
  - Paul Oswald Ahnert, German astronomer (b. 1897)
  - Konrad Lorenz, Austrian zoologist, recipient of the Nobel Prize in Physiology or Medicine (b. 1903)

March

- March 3 – Kenneth Hegan, English amateur footballer, professional soldier (b. 1901)
- March 6 – Harry Andrews, British actor (b. 1911)
-

- March 8
  - Robert Lacoste, French politician (b. 1898)
  - Carl Stuart Hamblen, American musician (b. 1908)
- March 9 – Robert Mapplethorpe, American photographer (b. 1946)
- March 10 – Maurizio Merli, Italian actor
- March 11 – James Kee, American politician (b. 1917)
- March 12 – Maurice Evans, English actor (b. 1901)
- March 14
  - Edward Abbey, American author and environmentalist (b. 1927)
  - Stephen D. Bechtel, Sr., American businessman (b. 1900)
  - Empress Zita of Bourbon-Parma, Wife of Emperor Charles I, last Empress of Austria (b. 1892)
- March 16 – Jesús María de Leizaola, Basque Spanish politician (b. 1896)
- March 17 – Merritt Butrick, American actor (b. 1959)
- March 19 – Alan Civil, English French horn player (b. 1929)
- March 21 – Milton Frome, American actor (b. 1909)
- March 27
  - May Allison, American actress (b. 1890)
  - Malcolm Cowley, American author (b. 1898)
  - Jack Starrett, American actor and director (b. 1936)
  - Scott Safran, Arcade game world record holder (b. 1967
- March 29
  - Bernard Blier, French actor (b. 1916)
  - Aleksandr Prokopenko, Soviet footballer (b. 1953)

April

Daphne du Maurier

Hamani Diori

Lucille Ball

Sergio Leone

- April 1 – George Robledo, Chilean soccer player (b. 1926)
- April 7 – Cheng Nan-jung, supporter of Taiwan independence movement (b.1947)
- April 9 – Moshe Ziffer, Israeli sculptor (b. 1902)
  - Gerald Flood, British actor (b. 1927)
  - Abbie Hoffman, American political activist (b. 1936)
  - Sugar Ray Robinson, American boxer (b. 1921)
- April 15
  - Hu Yaobang, General Secretary of the Communist Party of China (b. 1915)

- Charles Vanel, French actor (b. 1892)
- April 16 – Jocko Conlan, baseball player and umpire (b. 1899)
- April 19 – Daphne du Maurier, English writer (b. 1907)
- April 21
  - Princess Deokhye of Korea (b. 1912)
  - James Kirkwood, Jr., American playwright (b. 1924)
- April 22 – Emilio G. Segrè, Italian physicist, Nobel Prize laureate (b. 1905)
- April 23
  - Hamani Diori, Nigerien politician, former President (b. 1916)
  - Hu Die, Chinese actress (b. 1907 or 1908)
- April 24 – Edgar Sanabria, Venezuelan lawyer, diplomat, and politician, former President (b. 1911)
- April 25 – George Coulouris, English actor (b. 1903)
- April 26 – Lucille Ball, American entertainer (b. 1911)
- April 27 – Konosuke Matsushita, Japanese industrialist (b. 1894)
- April 30
  - Sergio Leone, Italian film director (b. 1929)
  - Bangja, Crown Princess Euimin of Korea (b. 1901)

May

Xiao Wangdong

- May 1 – Sally Kirkland, fashion editor at *Life* magazine (b. 1912)
- May 3 – Christine Jorgensen, transgender actress, singer, and writer (b. 1926)
- May 7 – Guy Williams, American actor (b. 1924)
- May 9 – Keith Whitley, American singer (b. 1955)

- May 10 – Woody Shaw, American jazz trumpeter (b. 1944)
- May 11 – Xiao Wangdong, Chinese general and Minister of Culture (b. 1910)
- May 15 – Johnny Green, American songwriter (b. 1908)
- May 16 – Leila Kasra, Iranian American poet (b. 1939)
- May 19
  - Anton Diffring, German actor (b. 1916)
  - C. L. R. James, Trinidadian writer and historian (b. 1901)
  - Robert Webber, American actor (b. 1924)
- May 20
  - John Hicks, English economist, Nobel Prize laureate (b. 1904)
  - Gilda Radner, American comedian and actress (b. 1946)
- May 26 – Don Revie, English footballer and manager (b. 1927)
- May 29 – John Cipollina, American musician (Quicksilver Messenger Service) (b. 1943)
- May 30 – James Harry Lacey, British World War II RAF Fighter pilot (b. 1917)
- May 31 – Edward Hubbard, British architectural historian, collaborator of the *Buildings of England* (b. 1937)

June

Ruhollah Khomeini

- June 3
  - Ayatollah Ruhollah Khomeini, Supreme Leader of Iran (b. 1902)
  - John McCauley, RAAF Senior Commander (b. 1899)
- June 4 – Dik Browne, American cartoonist (b. 1917)

- June 7 – Don the Beachcomber, American restaurateur (b. 1907)
- June 9
  - George Wells Beadle, American geneticist, recipient of the Nobel Prize in Physiology or Medicine (b. 1903)
  - Karl Skytte, Danish politician (b. 1908)
  - José López Rega, Argentine Peronist politician (b. 1916)
- June 10 – Richard Quine, American actor (b. 1920)
- June 13 – Fran Allison, actress (b. 1907)
- June 15
  - Ray McAnally, Irish actor (b. 1926)
  - Victor French, American actor and director (b. 1934)
- June 17 – John Matuszak, American football player and actor (b. 1950)
- June 22
  - Lee Calhoun, American Olympic athlete (b. 1933)
  - Menahem Stern, Israeli historian (b. 1925)
- June 23 – Werner Best, German Nazi official (b. 1903)
- June 24 – Hibari Misora, Japanese singer (b. 1937)
- June 26 – Howard Charles Green, Canadian politician, former Foreign secretary (b. 1895)
- June 27
  - Alfred Ayer, British philosopher (b. 1910)
  - Jack Buetel, American actor (b. 1915)
  - Michele Lupo, Italian film director (b. 1932)
- June 28 – Joris Ivens, Dutch filmmaker (b. 1898)

July

János Kádár

Mel Blanc

Laurence Olivier

Herbert von Karajan

- July 2
  - Andrei Gromyko, Soviet politician and diplomat, former Foreign Minister (b. 1909)
  - Hilmar Baunsgaard, Danish politician, former Prime Minister (b. 1920)
  - Ben Wright, English actor in radio, film and television (b. 1915)
  - Franklin Schaffner, American film director (b. 1920)
- July 3 – Jim Backus, American actor (b. 1913)
-

- July 4
  - Jack Haig, English actor (b. 1913)
  - Vic Perrin, American voice actor (b. 1916)
- July 6 – János Kádár, Hungarian politician & communist leader (b. 1912)
- July 10 – Mel Blanc, American voice actor best known for voicing characters like Bugs Bunny, Daffy Duck and Barney Rubble (b. 1908)
- July 11 – Laurence Olivier, English stage and screen actor and director (b. 1907)
- July 15 – Laurie Cunningham, English footballer (b. 1956)
- July 16 – Herbert von Karajan, Austrian conductor (b. 1908)
- July 17 – Itubwa Amram, Nauruan pastor and politician (b. 1922)
- July 18
  - Donnie Moore, baseball player (b. 1954)
  - Rebecca Schaeffer, American actress (b. 1967)
- July 19 – Kazimierz Sabbat, Polish president (b. 1913)
- July 20
  - Forrest H. Anderson, American politician (b. 1913)
  - Mary Treen, American film actress (b. 1907)
- July 22 – Martti Talvela, Finnish bass (b. 1935)
- July 23
  - Donald Barthelme, American writer (b. 1931)
  - Michael Sundin, English television presenter (b. 1961)
- July 24 – Ernie Morrison, American actor (b. 1912)
- July 30 – Lane Frost, American bull rider (b. 1963)

August

William Shockley

- August 1 – John Ogdon, English pianist (b. 1937)
- August 4
  - Maurice Colbourne, British actor (b. 1939)
  - Franziska Liebing, Swedish actress (b. 1901)
- August 7 – Mickey Leland, American congressman (b. 1944)
- August 12 – William Shockley, American physicist, Nobel Prize laureate (b. 1910)
- August 13
  - Hugo del Carril, Argentine film actor, film director and tango singer (b. 1912)
  - Tim Richmond, American race car driver (b. 1955)
- August 14 – Robert Bernard Anderson, American political figure (b. 1910)
- August 15 – Minoru Genda, Japanese aviator, naval officer, and politician (b. 1904)
- August 16
  - Jean-Hilaire Aubame, French-Gabonese politician (b. 1912)
  - Amanda Blake, American actress (b. 1929)
- August 17
  - Harry Corbett OBE, British TV presenter, creator of Sooty; (b. 1918)
  - Lin Tie, Chinese politician, head of Hebei province (b. 1904)
- August 20
  - George Adamson, Indian-born conservationist (assassinated) (b. 1906)
  - H. B. Halicki, American actor, stunt driver and filmmaker (b. 1940)
  - Joseph LaShelle, American cinematographer (b. 1900)
- August 21 – Raul Seixas, Brazilian singer (b. 1945)
- August 22
  - John Clyne, Canadian jurist (b. 1902)
  - Diana Vreeland, American fashion editor (b. 1929)
  - Huey P. Newton, co-founder of the Black Panther Party (murdered) (b. 1942)
- August 23 – R. D. Laing, Scottish psychiatrist (b. 1927)
- August 26 – Irving Stone, American writer (b. 1903)

- August 29 – Sir Peter Scott, English naturalist, artist, and explorer (b. 1909)
- August 30 – Joe Collins, baseball player (b. 1922)

September

Ferdinand Marcos

- September 1 – A. Bartlett Giamatti, American President of Yale University and MLB Commissioner (b. 1938)
- September 4
  - Georges Simenon, Belgian writer (b. 1903)
  - Ronald Syme, New Zealand-born classicist and historian (b. 1903)
- September 5
  - Les Allen, Australian footballer (b. 1911)
  - William Mann, English music critic (b. 1924)
- September 8
  - Ann George, English actress (b. 1903)
  - Paul Alfred Weiss, Austrian biologist (b. 1898)
- September 14 – Dámaso Pérez Prado, Cuban musician (b. 1916)
- September 15 – Robert Penn Warren, American writer (b. 1905)
- September 17
  - Hugh Quincy Alexander, American politician (b. 1911)
  - Steven Stayner, American kidnapping victim (b. 1965)
- September 22 – Irving Berlin, American composer (b. 1888)
- September 23 – Bradley Kincaid, American singer (b. 1894)
- September 28 – Ferdinand Marcos, former President of the Philippines (b. 1917)

- September 30
  - Horace Alexander, English writer, pacifist, and ornithologist (b. 1889)
  - Virgil Thomson, American composer (b. 1896)
  - Huỳnh Tấn Phát, Vietnamese politician (b. 1913)

October

Bette Davis

- October 4 – Graham Chapman, English comedian (*Monty Python*) (b. 1941)
- October 6 – Bette Davis, American actress (b. 1908)
- October 9 – Penny Lernoux, American journalist and author (b. 1940)
- October 11
  - M. King Hubbert, American geophysicist (b. 1903)
  - Paul Shenar, American actor (b. 1936)
- October 12 – Jay Ward, animator, creator of *Rocky and Bullwinkle*, *Dudley Do-Right*, etc. (b. 1920)
- October 16
  - Scott O'Dell, children's writer and winner of 5 Newbery Awards (b. 1898)
  - Cornel Wilde, American actor (b. 1915)
- October 20
  - Dahn Ben-Amotz, Israeli journalist and author (b. 1924)
  - Anthony Quayle, English actor (b. 1913)
- October 22
  - Jacob Wetterling, American kidnapping victim (b. 1978)
  - Roland Winters, American actor (b. 1904)

- October 25 – Mary McCarthy, American writer (b. 1912)
- October 26 – Charles J. Pedersen, American chemist, Nobel Prize laureate (b. 1904)
- October 30 – Pedro Vargas, Mexican singer and actor (b. 1904)
- October 31 – Georgi Partsalev, Bulgarian theatre and film actor (b. 1925)

November

Franz Joseph II

- November 1 – Sadie Tanner Mossell Alexander, American civil rights activist (b. 1898)
- November 3 – Timoci Bavadra, Fiji physician and politician (b. 1934)
- November 5 – Vladimir Horowitz, Russian pianist (b. 1903)
- November 5 – Barry Sadler, American soldier and singer-songwriter (b. 1940)
- November 11 – Kenneth MacLean Glazier, Sr., Canadian minister and librarian (b. 1912)
- November 13
    - Victor Davis, Canadian Olympic swimmer (b. 1964)
    - Franz Joseph II, 14th Sovereign Prince of Liechtenstein (b. 1906)
- November 20 – Lynn Bari, American actress (b. 1913)
- November 22
    - C. C. Beck, American cartoonist (b. 1910)
    - René Moawad, President of Lebanon (assassinated) (b. 1925)
- November 25 – George Cakobau, Fiji Governor General (b. 1912)

- November 26 – Ahmed Abdallah, Comorian politician, President of the Republic (assassinated) (b. 1919)
- November 27 – Carlos Arias Navarro, Spanish politician, former President of the Government (b. 1908)
- November 29 – Gubby Allen, English cricketer (b. 1902)
- November 30 – Ahmadou Ahidjo, Cameroonian politician, former President (b. 1924)

December

Andrei Sakharov

Lee Van Cleef

Samuel Beckett

Nicolae Ceauşescu

- December 1 – Alvin Ailey, American dancer and choreographer (b. 1931)
- December 2 – Ray Morehart, American baseball player (b. 1899)
- December 3
    - Sourou-Migan Apithy, Beninese political figure, former president of Dahomey (b. 1913)
    - Fernando Martín, Spanish basketball player (car accident) (b. 1962)
- December 4 – Frederick Elwyn Jones, British barrister and Labour politician (b. 1909)
- December 5 – John Pritchard, English conductor (b. 1921)
- December 6
    - Frances Bavier, American actress (b. 1902)
    - Sammy Fain, American composer (b. 1902)
    - Marc Lépine, Canadian mass murderer (b. 1964)
    - John Payne, American actor (b. 1912)
- December 7 – Haystacks Calhoun, American professional wrestler (b. 1934)
- December 8 – Hans Hartung, German-French painter (b. 1904)
- December 11 – Lindsay Crosby, American singer and actor (b. 1938)
- December 14
    - Jock Mahoney, American actor (b. 1919)
    - Andrei Sakharov, Russian physicist and activist, recipient of the Nobel Peace Prize (declined) (b. 1921)

- December 15 – Edward Underdown, stage and film veteran (b. 1908)
- December 16
  - Silvana Mangano, Italian actress (b. 1930)
  - Aileen Pringle, American actress (b. 1895)
- December 16 – Lee Van Cleef, American actor (b. 1925)
- December 17 – Albert C. Wedemeyer, American general (b. 1897)
- December 19
  - Kirill Mazurov, Belarusian Soviet politician (b. 1914)
  - Herbert Blaize, Prime Minister of Grenada (b. 1918)
- December 20 – Kurt Böhme, German bass (b. 1908)
- December 21
  - Ján Cikker, Slovak composer (b. 1911)
  - Rotimi Fani-Kayode, Nigerian/British photographer, co-founder Autograph ABP (b. 1955)
- December 22
  - Samuel Beckett, Irish writer, Nobel Prize laureate (b. 1906)
  - Vasile Milea, Romanian military officer and politician, minister of Defense (suicide) (b. 1927)
- December 25
  - Nicolae Ceaușescu, Romanian dictator, Communist Party head and President of the Republic (executed) (b. 1918)
  - Elena Ceaușescu, wife of Nicolae Ceaușescu and Deputy Prime Minister of Romania (executed) (b. 1916)
  - Billy Martin, American baseball player and manager (b. 1928)
- December 26 – Lennox Berkeley, English composer (b. 1903)
- December 30
  - Yasuji Miyazaki, Japanese Olympic swimmer (b. 1916)
  - Madoline Thomas, Welsh actress (b. 1890)
- December 31
  - Gerhard Schröder, German politician (b. 1910)
  - Sir Ignatius Kilage, 4th Governor-General of Papua New Guinea (b. 1941)

Nobel Prizes

- Physics – Norman F. Ramsey, Hans G. Dehmelt, Wolfgang Paul
- Chemistry – Sidney Altman, Thomas R. Cech
- Medicine – J. Michael Bishop, Harold E. Varmus
- Literature – Camilo José Cela
- Peace – Tenzin Gyatso, 14th Dalai Lama
- Cage of Sweden Prize in Economic Sciences in Memory of Alfred Nobel – Trygve Haavelmo

In the News

Sky TV Launched In UK.

The Galileo Spacecraft is launched by NASA.

Serial killer Ted Bundy is executed in Florida's electric chair.

A UK 747 crashes on the M1 Motorway.

Hillsborough disaster occurred on April 15th , 1989, at Hillsborough, a football stadium in Sheffield, England, resulting in the loss of 96 lives.

Nintendo begin selling the Game Boy.

Voyager II passes the planet Neptune and its moon Triton.

Popular Films - Batman, Indiana Jones and the Last Crusade, Lethal Weapon 2, Twins, Back to the Future Part II, Ghostbusters II.

First release of Microsoft Office.

Marchioness pleasure boat collides with a barge on the River Thames adjacent to Southwark Bridge and 51 die.

Leona Helmsley the billionaire hotel operator is convicted on Tax Fraud Charges.

In Egypt, a 4,400-year-old mummy is found in the Great Pyramid of Giza.

George Bush Snr becomes president of the United States.

The Berlin Wall comes down.

USSR pulls out of Afghanistan.

Scientists pronounce 1989 as the warmest on record.